W9-AZL-205

# *Daniel Boone*

## FRONTIER EXPLORER

# *Daniel Boone*

## FRONTIER EXPLORER

By Keith Brandt and
JoAnn Early Macken
Illustrated by John Lawn

SCHOLASTIC INC.
New York   Toronto   London   Auckland   Sydney
Mexico City   New Delhi   Hong Kong   Buenos Aires

No part of this publication may be reproduced, stored in a retrieval system, or transmitted in any form or by any means, electronic, mechanical, photocopying, recording, or otherwise, without written permission of the publisher. For information regarding permission, write to Scholastic Inc., Attention: Permissions Department, 557 Broadway, New York, NY 10012.

ISBN-13: 978-0-439-02020-6

ISBN-10: 0-439-02020-4

Copyright © 2008 by Scholastic Inc.

All rights reserved. Published by Scholastic Inc.

SCHOLASTIC and associated logos are trademarks and/or registered trademarks of Scholastic Inc.

12 11 10 9 8 7 6 5 4          9 10 11 12 13/0

Printed in the U.S.A.

First printing, January 2008

# CONTENTS

A Family on the Move     1

Wandering and Working     5

Learning to Hunt     11

Summers in the Pasture     17

Bear Tracks     22

Learning His Lessons     27

Wilderness Guide     30

Two Wars and a Family     35

Florida and Kentucky     40

The Wilderness Road     44

Index     51

# Daniel Boone

## FRONTIER EXPLORER

# CHAPTER 1:
## *A Family on the Move*

Some people like to stay in one place all their lives. They do not like change. They are afraid of new ideas and of being different from others. For them, the old ways are the best.

Other people love the challenges of new ideas and new places. They follow their own beliefs, even when that way is unpopular. George and Mary Boone were such people.

Leaving England for the American colonies in the early 1700s was a huge challenge. But that did not stop the Boones and their nine children from making the dangerous ocean crossing. They looked forward to their new life in Pennsylvania. They had heard that the land there was cheap and plentiful, and that it produced fine crops. The woods were said to be filled with wild game. The Boones knew that life on the frontier would not be easy. But they also believed that anyone willing to work hard could live a good life in the bountiful new land.

The Boones also looked forward to practicing their Quaker religion freely. In England, Quakers were treated harshly for their beliefs. Such practices would not occur in Pennsylvania.

Three of the older Boone children crossed the ocean first. Two brothers and a sister reached their new country in 1713. Four years later, the rest of the family followed.

Soon after landing in the colonies, the family traveled to Oley Township, in what is

now Pennsylvania. Oley was a new settlement at the edge of the wilderness. There, George Boone built a sturdy stone house for his family. He cleared many of his four hundred acres of land for farming. Soon, he was a leading citizen in the colony. He donated land to build the Oley Meeting House for the local Quaker community. He also became a justice of the peace. A hardworking, fair, and honorable man, George was well respected in Oley, as were his children.

George's son, Squire, was one of the first members of the family to arrive in the colonies. He was a small, fair man with red hair and blue-gray eyes. Squire Boone had learned two trades. He was both a weaver and a blacksmith. In 1720, he married Sarah Morgan, a large, strong woman with dark eyes and black hair. They settled on land near his father's. All his brothers and sisters lived nearby.

Squire and Sarah raised crops and livestock. With help from friends and neighbors, they built a one-room log cabin. The house stood on a rock ledge near a spring. Daniel Boone was born there on October 22, 1734. He was the sixth of Sarah and Squire's eleven children.

# CHAPTER 2:
## *Wandering and Working*

Much of what is said about Daniel Boone is folklore. People like hearing stories about his great adventures, so they are often told. Some tales have grown a little taller with each telling. Most people agree, though, that Daniel Boone was always a wanderer.

Even as a child, he could not stay still for long. At home, he had plenty of space to roam. He could ramble through the cornfields, into the woods, or down to the shallow stream and still be safe.

Daniel's parents never worried much about his wanderings. He had a wonderful sense of direction. Even if he went deep into the woods, he would be sure to find his way home before supper. It was as if he had been born with a magical gift for navigation.

Daniel was an easy child to raise—as long as he wasn't asked to stay indoors. He was bright, good-tempered, strong, and not at all lazy. But once a month, the Quakers held services at their Meeting House. These

meetings might have lasted for hours, and sitting still for so long must have been hard for Daniel.

When Daniel was quite young, a smallpox epidemic struck the area. His mother kept all the children in the house so they would not catch the disease. Daniel could not stand being stuck inside. He and his sister Elizabeth made a plan. They thought that if they caught the disease, they would be allowed back outside when they were healthy again.

One night, they crept out of the house. They visited friends who were sick with smallpox. Daniel and Elizabeth even climbed into their sick friends' beds with them! Mrs. Boone was angry, but both Boone children survived the illness. And after that, they could play outside again.

Daniel enjoyed doing any work that took him outdoors. He often helped out in his father's blacksmith shop. There, he learned how to fix his own traps.

Young Daniel learned to do many chores on the Boone farm. In those days, frontier boys had to know how to plow the fields, plant corn and vegetables, and harvest the crops. They cut hay and stacked it in neat piles. They cut down trees and chopped them into firewood, split logs into boards, built cabins, and made furniture.

Daniel also learned how to tend the farm animals. He needed to know how to make

tools, dig a well, and repair anything inside and outside the house. He had to make and set traps to catch wild animals. Daniel's father believed a frontier boy should learn every skill he could, and Daniel was a willing and able learner.

# CHAPTER 3:
## *Learning to Hunt*

As a Quaker, Daniel was taught to stay out of arguments. He did not like to fight. He did like to swim, run, and wrestle with his cousins and friends. He spent a lot of free time with his best friend, Henry Miller. Henry worked in Daniel's father's forge.

The boys often set off into the woods with bows and arrows. It was important for them to know how to shoot straight—to have a steady hand and a keen eye. Daniel and his friends often held archery contests. One day, the target might be a thick oak tree fifty yards away. Another day, they might aim at a birch sapling thirty yards away. Sometimes they tossed a corncob into the air and tried to shoot an arrow into it.

Most people missed targets like that, but Daniel did not. He had a natural talent for shooting. With a bow and arrow, Daniel Boone was the best target shooter in his part of the country.

The boys also used their bows and arrows for hunting. The woods were full of rabbits, squirrels, turkeys, and other wild game. Whatever the boys shot, they brought home for dinner. Daniel, who could glide through the trees in silence, always managed to bring something back.

When Daniel went into the woods, he tried to think of himself as an Indian. For as long as Daniel could remember, he had admired Indians. They hunted better than any settler he knew. They knew which plants were safe

to eat and which ones to use as medicine. And they loved the wilderness the way he did.

The Shawnee and Delaware Indians in the area came to know and like the Boone boy. He treated them with respect. He asked them questions, listened carefully to what they said, and was happy to learn from them.

In return, they were willing to teach him and answer his questions.

The Indians taught Daniel to walk through the forest as they did, without leaving a trace. They taught him to follow the nearly invisible trails left by deer traveling through the woods. From the Indians, Daniel learned how to move so

swiftly and quietly that even animals could not sense he was near.

The Indians also taught Daniel how to hide downwind at a pond. Animals coming to drink could not see or smell him. The frontier boy was thrilled to watch deer, rabbits, and other animals come close to his hiding place and know they had no idea he was there.

# CHAPTER 4:
## *Summers in the Pasture*

When Daniel was ten, his father bought twenty-five acres of rich pasture land. There, cows could graze, grow fat, and give plenty of milk. Mr. Boone planned to use most of the milk to make butter and cheese to sell.

This new pasture was four or five miles away from the Boone family's farm. The cows had to stay there all summer, so someone had to live there to take care of them. Mr. Boone built a small log cabin at the edge of the pasture. Mrs. Boone and Daniel moved

in for the summer. Every morning at sunrise, Daniel turned the cows loose. They grazed contentedly all day. At sundown, the boy rounded up the herd and brought them back to the cabin for milking.

Mrs. Boone churned the milk into butter and made cheese. Once a week, someone brought the cheese and butter back home. Some weeks, Daniel's brothers rode out from the farm. They brought family news, local gossip, fruit and vegetables, and supplies. They returned with the butter and cheese. Other weeks, Mrs. Boone brought the butter and cheese home. Then Daniel was happy to be left on his own for a while.

Daniel and his mother spent six summers this way. Some years, his younger brothers and sisters may have come along. Later, he remembered these months as the best times of his life. His love for the wilderness and the life of a hunter began then.

Except for helping with the cows, Daniel was free all day. He did some hunting with his bow and arrow, but mostly he hunted with a special weapon he made himself. Daniel would pull a young sapling from the soil, roots and all. He stripped off the bark and broke off the branches. He made a thin club with a round knob of roots at one end, and he practiced throwing it at trees and rocks.

When his aim was close to perfect, he took his weapon hunting.

At first, he missed many moving targets. But Daniel kept at it. Soon he pitched his club so well that he could hit rabbits and squirrels from far away.

# CHAPTER 5:
# *Bear Tracks*

For Daniel's twelfth birthday, his parents gave him his first rifle. This was a proud and important day for Daniel. He knew his parents saw him as a young man ready to accept responsibility.

Daniel later remembered that rifle as the best gift anyone ever gave him. From that day on, Daniel was the family's best hunter. When the Boones needed fresh meat, Mrs. Boone sent Daniel out for it, and he always came back with enough for everyone.

Daniel was such a sure shot and a clever

woodsman that his mother didn't worry much about his safety. He began to take longer winter trips to hunt in the nearby hills and mountains. But one summer evening, when Daniel was about thirteen, he didn't bring the cows home for milking. At first, Mrs.

Boone just shook her head. She was certain she would see her son by bedtime, so she fetched the cows herself.

When Daniel still wasn't back the next morning, Mrs. Boone began to worry. Maybe he fell and broke a leg, she thought. Maybe he ran into a wildcat. Something had to be wrong!

Mrs. Boone told her husband, and he gathered a search party. For days, they looked for Daniel, but they could not find a trace of him. Mr. Boone knew his son could move through the forest like a shadow and not leave a trail. But he must have wished Daniel wasn't quite so good at it this time!

At last, several days after the boy disappeared, the searchers saw a wisp of smoke in the distance. At nightfall, they reached its source. They found a shelter made of bark, like the ones the Indians built. Inside it, Daniel sat on a bearskin, roasting a chunk of bear meat over a fire. The rest of the meat was

cut up and hanging on branches outside.

"Were you lost?" Mr. Boone asked his son.

"Lost?" Daniel asked, grinning. "No, sir. We're on the south side of Neversink Mountain, maybe nine miles from the cow pasture."

"Why are you here?" Mr. Boone asked. "Your mother has been sick with worry."

"I'm sorry I gave her cause for worry," Daniel said. "I got to tracking this bear. He kept going, so I kept going. My mind was set on bringing him back. I think she'll be pleased to see all this meat."

"I think she'll be more pleased to see you!" Mr. Boone said. And, of course, she was.

# CHAPTER 6:
# *Learning His Lessons*

By the time he reached his teens, Daniel was known far and wide as the finest shot and woodsman in Pennsylvania. He had pale skin and blue-gray eyes like his father's. He had dark hair like his mother's, and he wore it in a long braid. He dressed in a belted jacket and pants made of deerskin with fringe along the sides. A hunting knife and a hatchet hung from his belt. In a bag on his shoulder, he carried bullets and a powder horn, a container for gunpowder made from an animal's horn. Although he is sometimes pictured in a raccoon skin cap, he preferred a tall black hat.

Daniel's only classroom was the outdoors. He once told his children he never attended a day of school in his life. In fact, he didn't learn to read and write until he was fourteen! His older brother Samuel's wife, Sarah, was his first teacher. She did the best she could, but Daniel was not a willing pupil.

Next, the boy's Uncle John, a local teacher, took on the job. He was no more successful. Daniel couldn't bear to sit indoors, and he struggled with his lessons. John Boone also gave up. He told Daniel's father the boy was hopeless as a student.

Mr. Boone just shrugged his shoulders. "It's all right, John," he said. "Let the girls do the spelling. Daniel will do the shooting, and between you and me, that is what we most need." In those days, many people could not read or write.

One night, Daniel and his friend Henry wanted to go to a party. They knew Daniel's strict Quaker parents would not allow them to go, so they snuck out of the cabin. They both rode off on Mr. Boone's horse.

On the way home, they thought they could jump the horse over a sleeping cow. At the last moment, the cow rose up. The horse stumbled and fell to the ground, its neck broken. The boys were not hurt, but the horse died. Terrified, the boys put the saddle back in the barn. They went to bed without saying a word. Mr. Boone never found out what happened to his horse.

# CHAPTER 7:
# *Wilderness Guide*

In 1750, when Daniel was fifteen, the Boones decided to move on. With so many settlers pouring into Pennsylvania, Mr. Boone felt crowded. Many of the forests were being cut down for new farmland, and hunters were wiping out the wild animals.

Mr. Boone's sister sent word from Virginia. Good, cheap land was available there. So Mr. Boone sold his land to a cousin. The family packed their pots and pans, farm tools, and a spinning wheel onto a wagon. They sold everything that didn't fit. Their horses pulled the wagon, and the cows followed behind. The family headed for the wilderness, not even sure where they would settle.

All the Boone children went along with their parents. Two married brothers brought their wives. One married sister brought her husband and their baby. Mr. Boone's nephew and Henry Miller also joined them.

Daniel guided the group. They must have driven at least three or four wagons. On a good day, they probably traveled about fifteen miles. Several weeks later, they settled in Virginia.

After a growing season or two, Daniel and Henry Miller left for a long hunt. They worked their way south to North Carolina. When they had as many animal skins as they could carry, they headed home. They stopped to visit Daniel's family, and then continued north to sell their hides and furs in Philadelphia. Within a few weeks, they had spent all the money they earned.

Daniel thought of that trip as a turning point. From then on, he rarely missed a fall hunt for the rest of his life. After that trip, Henry Miller settled down, bought land, and started an ironworks. Daniel didn't see him again for thirty years.

The stories Daniel and Henry told of the beautiful mountains, the clear and sparkling streams, the rich soil, and the plentiful wild game made the Boones pack up and move once more. In 1751, they reached western North Carolina. They settled in the valley of the Yadkin River.

The Boones cut down trees and cleared a place in the woods. Mr. Boone built a log cabin on a creek at a spot called Buffalo Lick. The new Boone home had plenty of large trees, fish to catch, and animals to hunt. The Boones plowed their land and planted corn and sweet potatoes. But while Daniel worked in the fields, he hoped for rain so he could go hunting instead.

Daniel often brought home meat for the family. During the winter, he trapped beaver, otter, and muskrat. One account says that he and a companion killed thirty deer in one day near the river. Daniel alone is said to have killed ninety-nine bears in one season along a nearby creek. It was later named Bear Creek after this feat.

As more Boone children married, each family settled on a plot of land nearby. But Daniel had no interest in farming. After he had lived in the wilderness, he wanted to keep moving.

# CHAPTER 8:

## *Two Wars and a Family*

Settlers kept pushing the Indians farther and farther west. Settlers cleared the forests for farming, so Indians could no longer hunt there. Settlers hunted the forestland that was left, so Indians found fewer animals for their food. Settlers bought land from the Indians, but many of the deals were unfair to the Indians. A deal might be made with one tribe for a place that was used by several tribes. The others were left with nothing.

At the same time, the French and the English were fighting over land. In 1754, when Daniel Boone was about twenty, the French and Indian War broke out. Some tribes joined the French soldiers fighting against the English and the colonial troops. Daniel joined the North Carolina militia. He drove a supply wagon and worked as a blacksmith.

After the war, Daniel met Rebecca Bryan, the daughter of a neighbor. Daniel had hunted with Rebecca's three brothers. Daniel and Rebecca went cherry picking. Later, he brought her family a deer he had killed.

Daniel and Rebecca were married in 1756. They built a home on Sugartree Creek and cleared some land for farming. The log house had one door and a huge stone fireplace. Outside stood a small kitchen for cooking in the summer. Daniel's two nephews, whose parents had died, moved in with them. The next year, their son James was born. Another son, Israel, was born in 1759, the second of their ten children.

Daniel worked as a blacksmith, but he wasn't done wandering. He continued to hunt, trap, and explore the wilderness, sometimes in the Appalachian Mountains and most often alone. As more settlers moved in, he traveled farther and farther into the mountains to find game. He was away from home longer and longer. He might spend weeks at a time with just his dog and his horse. He often carried a Bible or a history book. *Gulliver's Travels* was his favorite book.

Daniel knew his way around so well that once he saw a place, he always knew it when he returned to it. He sometimes carved messages into the bark of trees. One famous carving marks a spot where he killed a bear. Another one points to water.

While Daniel was gone, Rebecca must have kept busy. Pioneer women had to cook and clean, spin and weave, wash and sew. They fetched water, chopped wood, and milked cows. They churned butter, tended gardens, and cared for their families. Their nearest neighbors might have been miles away.

Daniel fought in the Cherokee War in about 1760. He hunted on land that became North Carolina, Virginia, and Tennessee. After two years, he returned home to his family. By then, more settlers had built homes in the valley. Daniel Boone began to think about moving again.

# CHAPTER 9:
## *Florida and Kentucky*

In 1765, Daniel traveled south to Florida. He made the journey with seven other men, planning to hunt as well as explore. The group found swamps full of insects but little game to hunt. Some Seminole Indians helped them and gave them food. The group returned through land that later became Alabama, Georgia, and South Carolina.

In 1767, Daniel set foot in Kentucky for the first time. A trader had told Daniel of a spot on the Ohio River in Kentucky where fat ducks and geese were swept over a waterfall and all a man had to do was pick them up. In Kentucky, Daniel hunted buffalo, got caught in a snowstorm, and stayed longer than he had planned.

Daniel led several other hunting trips into Kentucky. One that began in May of 1769 included five other men and ten or fifteen horses. The horses carried tools, traps, blankets, and food. The men hunted for eight months, killing buffalo, elk, and many deer. Each man had hundreds of skins, worth about a dollar apiece, and each horse could carry about one hundred skins. The skins had to be scraped with knives, dried, and then rubbed across a board to make them soft.

The men hunted on Shawnee Indian hunting land. But the Indians needed this land to hunt for their own food. They were angry because the settlers took only the animal skins and left the meat to spoil. One group of Shawnee took the hunters' horses and all the skins and told the hunters to go home.

Most of the hunters gave up, but Daniel stayed on, hunting and exploring alone. One day, another group of hunters was startled to find him lying on the ground, singing.

Daniel spent three months on his own before his brother Squire showed up with supplies. He stayed to hunt for a while, too. Squire made two trips home to sell loads of skins. But before he could make a third trip, a group of angry Indians took all the skins. By the time Daniel finally returned home in May of 1771, he had been gone so long that his own family did not know him.

Although he did not make much money from his Kentucky hunting trips, Daniel knew the country better than any other settler did. He knew the best farming and hunting lands. He knew where the land was too rocky for farming. And he knew where spring rains turned the soil to swamp.

By this time, settlers had pushed far beyond the limits set by their treaties with the Indians. The Indians kept giving up more land, but it was never enough for the settlers. Tensions rose because both sides believed they were right. Travel became more dangerous. Some on each side worked for peace, but others fought at every chance.

In 1773, Daniel led a group of families who planned to settle in Kentucky. His own family was among them. A small group sent back for more supplies was attacked by Indians. Daniel's sixteen-year-old son, James, was among those killed. The whole group turned back in sorrow. It must have been hard for Daniel to fight the Indians after he came to know and respect them as friends and teachers.

# CHAPTER 10:

# *The Wilderness Road*

In 1775, a North Carolina company made a deal with a group of Cherokee Indians. The company wanted to buy twenty million acres of rich Kentucky land. The company owners planned to sell parcels of land to settlers. But making treaties with Indians, especially about land, was against the law for private citizens. The company had no legal right to make the deal.

Not all the Cherokee agreed to the terms. Besides, other tribes also used the land.

But the company went ahead with the sale anyway. The payment was six wagons full of goods, including guns, liquor, blankets, clothing, and tools. Daniel helped spread the word among the Indians, and more than a thousand Indians showed up to share the goods.

The deal also included the right to build a road into the territory and start a settlement there. The company chose Daniel to lead the way. He left in March 1775 with about thirty men. Two women came along to cook for them.

Cutting a road through the wild, beautiful land was hard work. Some days, the pioneers covered a good distance. Other days, rainy weather slowed their progress to a crawl. They crossed deep, rocky ravines and chopped their way through dense forests. Huge trees took hours to bring down.

Indians killed several members of this

group. Some of the pioneers turned back, and others joined the party. Daniel led them down Otter Creek to a spot on the south bank of the Kentucky River. Huge sycamore trees stood all around. Deer and buffalo gathered at a salt lick nearby, making the place ideal for hunting. Daniel chose this spot for the settlement.

The first building was a fort named Fort Boone in honor of Daniel. The settlers soon built a number of cabins there. They cleared and planted fields. Families began to arrive then. Daniel brought his own family there to live. More settlers soon came and, before long, a town had grown in the wilderness. Daniel was honored again when the town was named Boonesborough.

The rough, winding trail the settlers carved to Boonesborough came to be known as the Wilderness Road. Later, the road was widened. Thousands of wagons followed the pioneers' trail.

The urge to be out there, in a world known only to Indians, was a part of Daniel all his life. Someone once asked Daniel if he had ever been lost. "No," he said, "I can't say as ever I was lost, but I was bewildered once for three days." In his later years, he traveled and trapped all over Missouri. He even volunteered to fight in the War of 1812 when he was seventy-eight years old!

By the time Daniel died, on September 26, 1820, he was a legend. He had spent almost every one of his nearly eighty-six years exploring the wilderness. Daniel Boone is remembered and admired as one of the greatest frontiersmen in American history.

# *Index*

American colonies, challenge of moving to,
     1–2
Animal skins, selling, 31–33

Bear, tracking and hunting, 23–26
Bear Creek, 34
Bear killing, 34
Blacksmith, working as, 38
Boone, Daniel
  death of, 49
  folklore about, 5–6
  hunting trips of, 38

Boone, Elizabeth, 7–8

Boone, George, 3–4

Boone, Israel, 36

Boone, James, 36, 43

Boone, John, 28

Boone, Sarah (brother's wife), 28

Boone, Squire, 4, 42

Boone family, move to American colonies,
    1–2

Boonesborough, road to, 46

Bryan, Rebecca (wife), 36, 38–39

Buffalo hunting, 41

Cherokee Indians, treaties with, 44–46

Cherokee War, 39

Childhood, 5–9

Children (Daniel Boone's), 36

Delaware Indians, 14–15

Farm work, 8–9
    on pasture lands, 17–21

Florida, journey to, 40

Forest, learning plants and animals of, 12–16

French and Indian War, 35–36

Hunting
  with first rifle, 22–24
  learning skills of, 11–16
  love for, 19–21
Hunting trips, to Kentucky, 40–43

Indians
  agreements and conflict with, 44–46
  learning from, 12–16
  settlers and, 43
  taking land from, 35

Kentucky, 40–43

Marriage, 36
Miller, Henry, 11, 31

Morgan (Boone), Sarah, 4
Mother, 17–19

North Carolina, move to, 33

Oley Meeting House, 3–4
Oley Township, 2–4
Otter Creek, 46
Outdoors as classroom, 27–29

Parents, 6
Pasture land, summers in, 17–21
Pennsylvania, Boones in, 2–4
Pioneer women, 38–39

Quaker meetings, 6–7
Quakers, 2–4, 11

Religious freedom, 2
Rifle, first, 22–24

School, outdoors as, 27–29
Settlers, 35
  taking Indian lands, 43
Shawnee Indians, 14–15
  hunting land of, 41–42
Smallpox epidemic, 7–8
Sugartree Creek home, 36

Target shooting, 12

Virginia, move to, 30–31

Wanderings, in early childhood, 5–6
War of 1812, 49
Wilderness
  exploring and settling, 43–49
  working as guide in, 30–34
Wilderness Road, building of, 44–47

Yadkin River valley, 33

Look for these other exciting
**EASY BIOGRAPHIES:**

*Abigail Adams*
*Elizabeth Blackwell*
*Davy Crockett*
*Marie Curie*
*Amelia Earhart*
*Thomas Edison*
*Albert Einstein*
*Benjamin Franklin*
*Helen Keller*
*Martin Luther King, Jr.*
*Abraham Lincoln*
*Rosa Parks*
*Harriet Tubman*
*George Washington*
*The Wright Brothers*